This list is dedicated to all those lighthouse lovers, who, like us, want to search out and see (and in our case, photograph), every standing lighthouse in the U.S.

We have spent many hours searching and researching and would have given anything if a list like this had existed when we started out on our quest.

16th Edition, Sept. 2001

© Copyright 1993-2001, by Bob & Sandra Shanklin

All rights reserved. No part of this book may be reproduced or transmitted in any form by any means, electronic or mechanical, including photocopying and recording, or by any information storage and retrieval systems, except as may be expressly permitted by the 1976 Copyright Act or by the publisher. Requests for permission should be made in writing to:

Bob & Sandra Shanklin
517 Thornhill Road
Fort Walton Beach, Florida 32547

ISBN 0-9677544-1-0

West Quoddy Head

INDEX

Hawaii

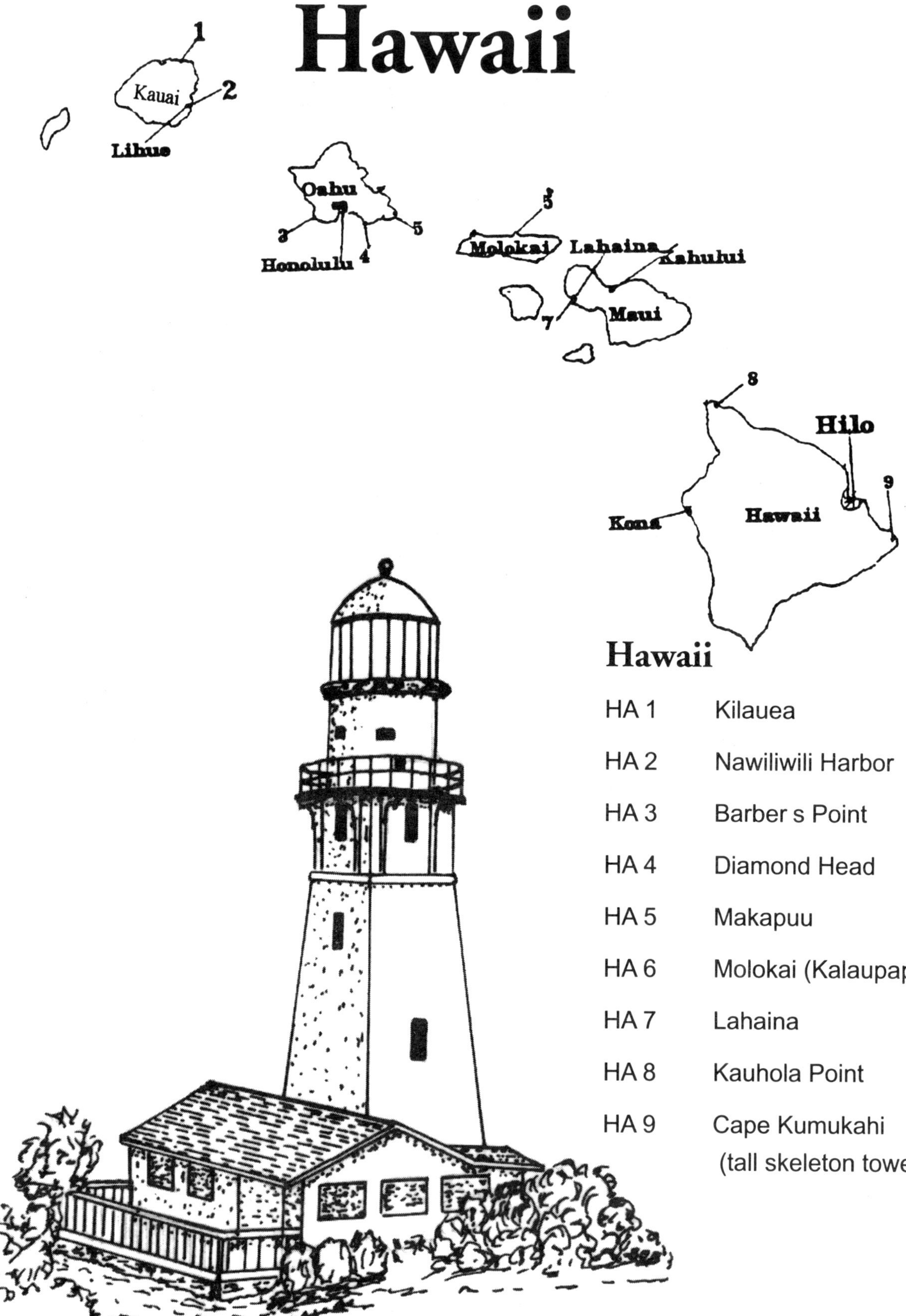

Hawaii

HA 1   Kilauea

HA 2   Nawiliwili Harbor

HA 3   Barber s Point

HA 4   Diamond Head

HA 5   Makapuu

HA 6   Molokai (Kalaupapa)

HA 7   Lahaina

HA 8   Kauhola Point

HA 9   Cape Kumukahi
        (tall skeleton tower)

Diamond Head

Alaska

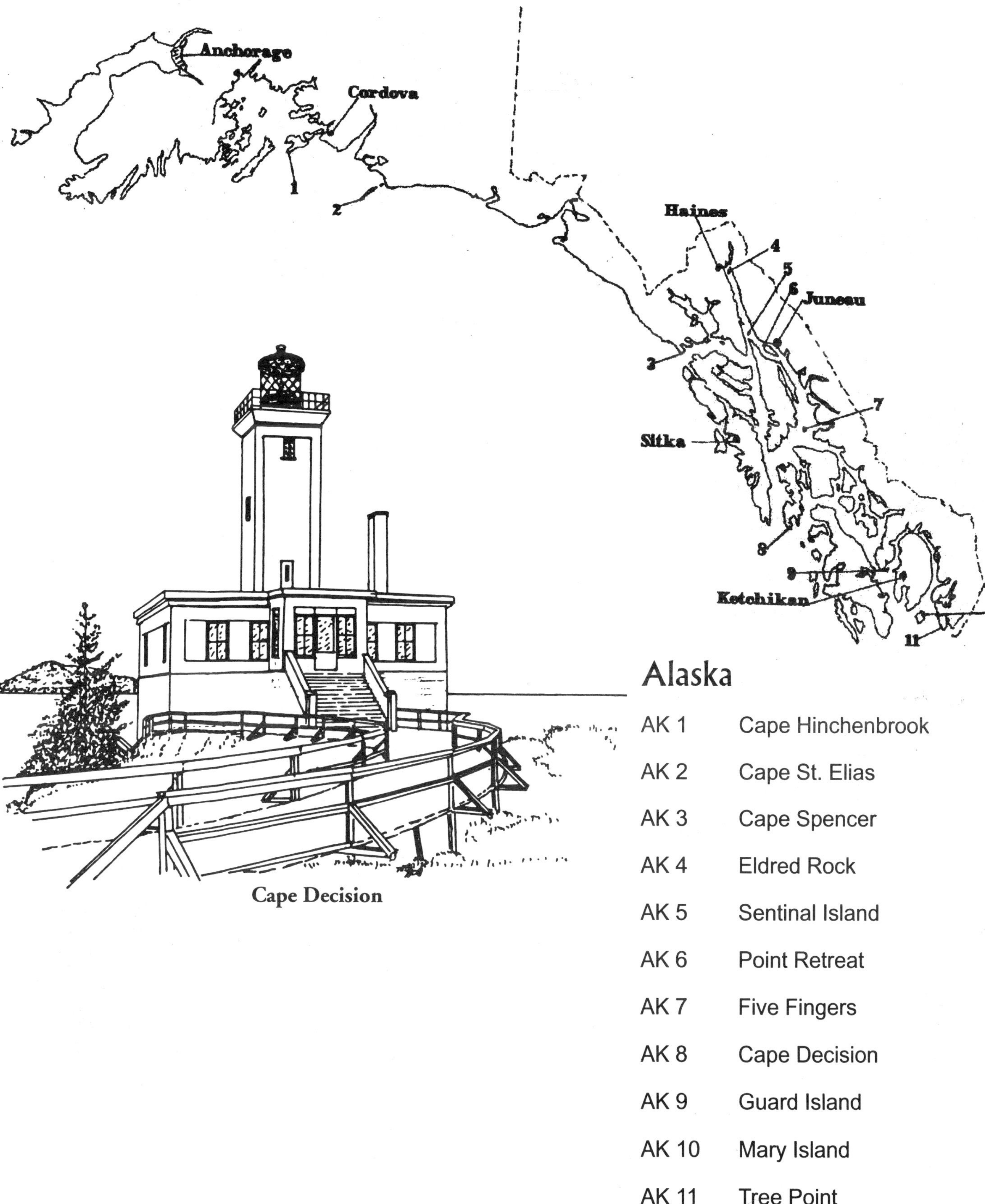

Cape Decision

Alaska

Washington

Lime Point

Oregon

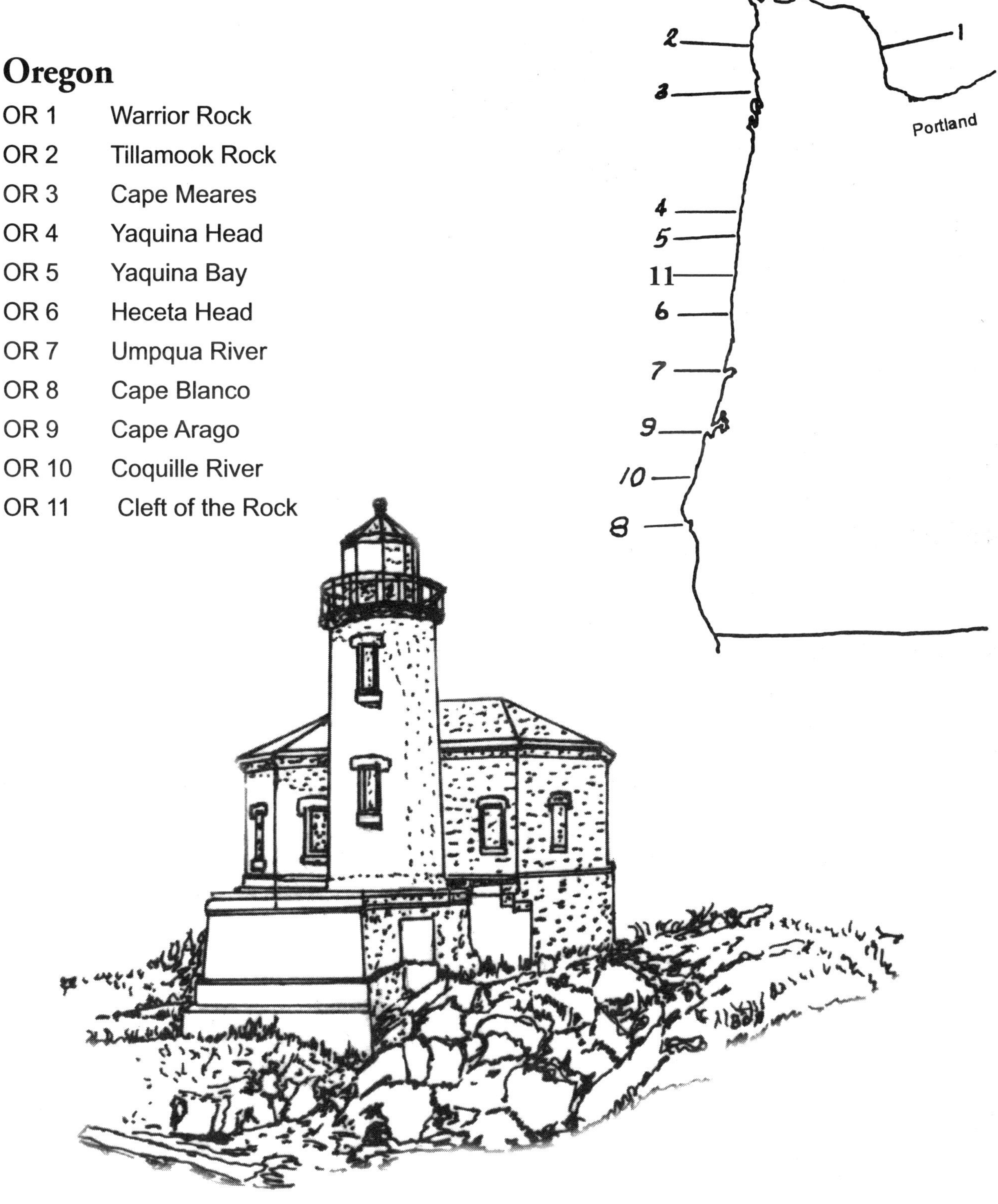

Coquille River

California

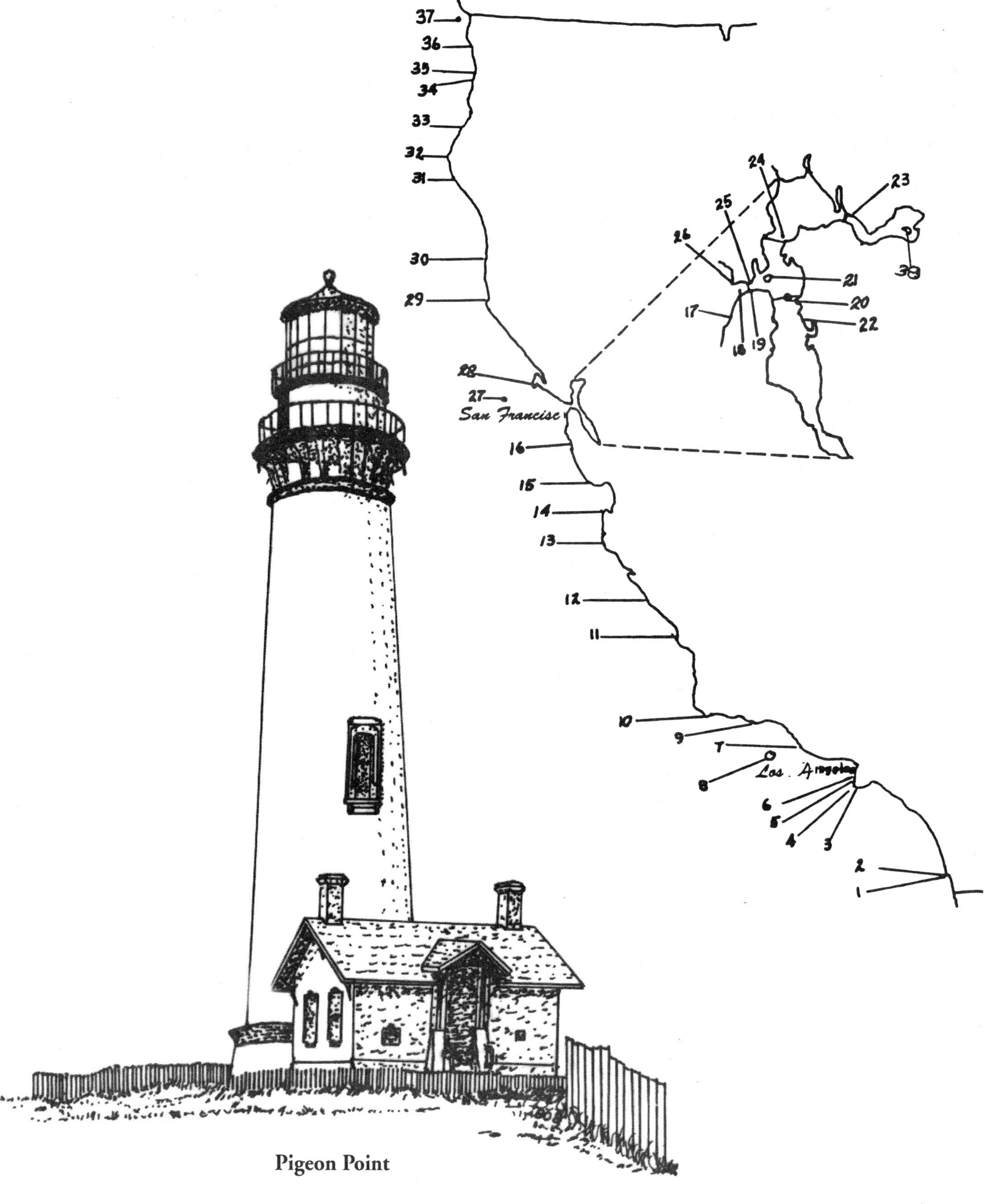

Pigeon Point

CA 1   Point Loma
CA 2   Old Point Loma
CA 3   Long Beach Harbor (the Robot Light)
CA 4   Los Angeles Harbor
CA 5   Point Fermin
CA 6   Point Vicente
CA 7   Port Hueneme
CA 8   Anacapa Island
CA 9   Santa Barbara, beacon on pyramid metal tower
CA 10   Point Conception
CA 11   Port St. Luis, San Luis Obispo
CA 12   Piedras Blancas
CA 13   Point Sur
CA 14   Point Pinos
CA 15   Santa Cruz, memorial lighthouse
CA 16   Pigeon Point
CA 17   Point Montara
CA 18   Mile Rock
CA 19   Fort Point
CA 20   Yerba Buena
CA 21   Alcatraz
CA 22   Old Oakland Harbor, relocated (Quinn s Restaurant)
CA 23   Old Carquinez Straits moved and now marina, no tower
CA 24   East Brother
CA 25   Lime Point
CA 26   Point Bonita
CA 27   Farallon Islands
CA 28   Point Reyes
CA 29   Point Arena
CA 30   Point Cabrillo
CA 31   Punta Gorda
CA 32   Cape Mendocino
CA 33   Old Table Bluff, tower only, restored & relocated
CA 34   Trinidad Head
CA 35   Memorial Lighthouse in Trinidad (replica)
CA 36   Battery Point, Crescent City
CA 37   St. George Reef
CA 38   Southampton Shoals, moved to Island near Stockton

Minnesota

Split Rock

Minnesota

MN 1	Grand Marais
MN 2	Split Rock
MN 3	Two Harbors
MN 4	Two Harbors Breakwater
MN 5	Duluth North Pier
MN 6	Duluth Breakwater Outer
MN 7	Duluth Breakwater Inner
MN 8	Minnesota Point, ruins, no top

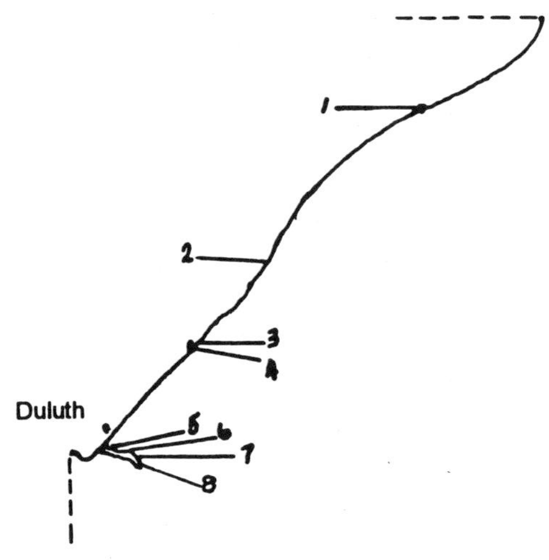

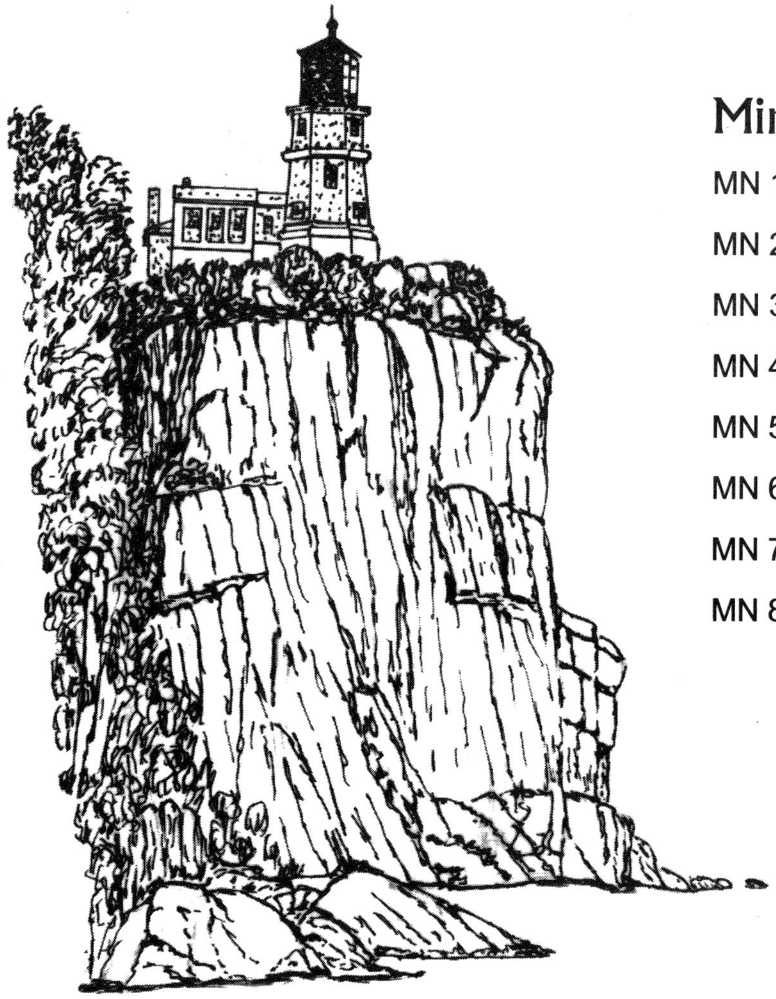

Wisconsin

Superior South Breakwater

WI 1	Superior South Breakwater
WI 2	Sand Island
WI 3	Devil s Island
WI 4	Outer Island
WI 5	Raspberry Island
WI 6	Michigan Island
WI 7	La Pointe
WI 8	Chequamegon Point
WI 9	Ashland Breakwater
WI 10	Long Tail Point, ruins, no top
WI 11	Grassy Island Range, a pair
WI 12	Kimberly
WI 13	Brays Point
WI 14	Fond Du Lac
WI 15	Pipe
WI 16	Green Bay Harbor Entrance
WI 17	Peshtigo Reef
WI 18	Sherwood Point
WI 19	Green Island, ruins, no tower
WI 20	Chamber s Island
WI 21	Eagle Bluff
WI 22	Plum Island Range
WI 23	Pilot Island
WI 24	Pottawatamie
WI 25	{ St. Martin Island &
WI 26	{ Poverty Island are actually in Mich.
WI 27	Cana Island
WI 28	Bailey s Harbor
WI 29	Bailey s Harbor Range
WI 30	Sturgeon Bay Canal
WI 31	Sturgeon Bay Canal N. Pierhead
WI 32	Algoma Pierhead
WI 33	Kewaunee Pierhead
WI 34	Rawley Point
WI 35	Two Rivers North Pierhead
WI 36	Manitowoc
WI 37	Sheboygan
WI 38	Port Washington Breakwater
WI 39	North Point
WI 40	Milwaukee Pierhead
WI 41	Milwaukee Breakwater
WI 42	Wind Point
WI 43	Racine N. Breakwater
WI 44	Kenosha Pierhead
WI 45	Old Kenosha Lighthouse (Southport)

Michigan

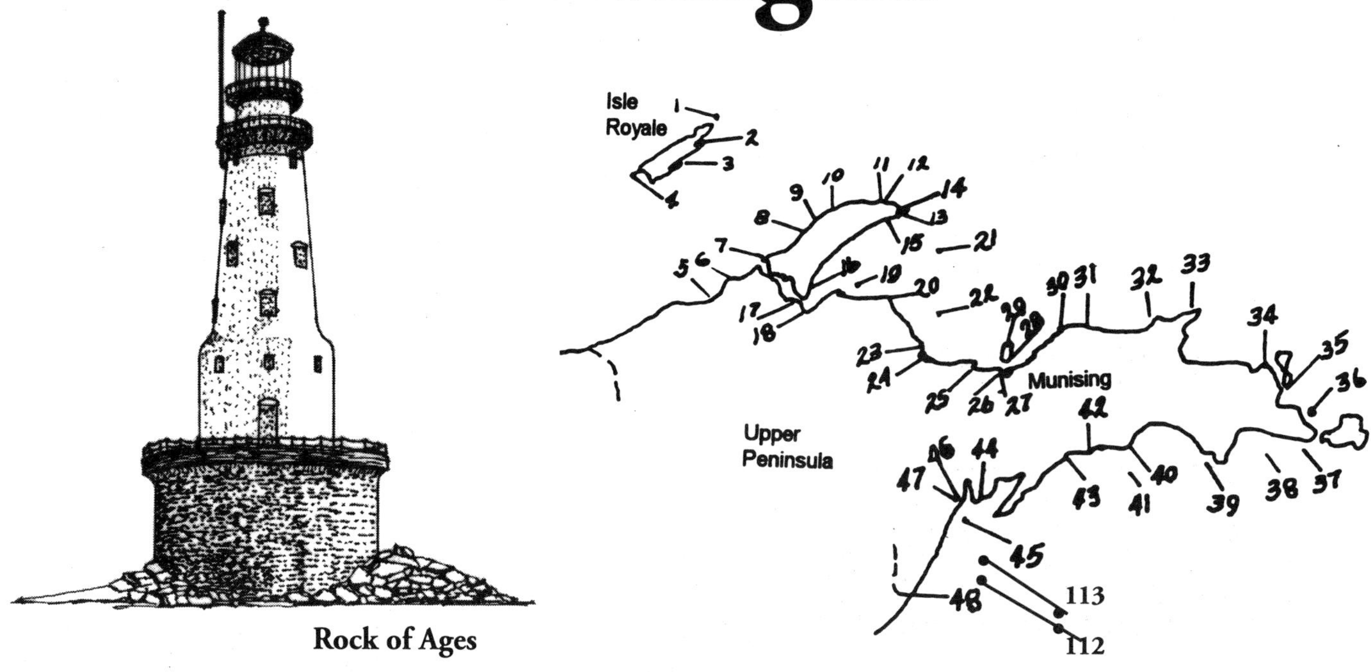

Rock of Ages

MI 1	Passage Island	MI 25	Grand Island Harbor Rear Range
MI 2	Rock Harbor	MI 26	Munising Rear Range
MI 3	Isle Royale	MI 27	Munising Front Range
MI 4	Rock of Ages	MI 28	Grand Island E. Channel
MI 5	Ontonogon	MI 29	Grand Island
MI 6	Fourteen Mile	MI 30	Au Sable
MI 7	Keweenau Upper Range	MI 31	Grand Marais Harbor Outer
MI 8	Sand Hills	MI 32	Crisp Point
MI 9	Eagle River	MI 33	Whitefish Point
MI 10	Eagle Harbor	MI 34	Point Iroquois
MI 11	Copper Harbor	MI 35	Cedar Point Rear Range, ruins
MI 12	Copper Harbor Rear Range	MI 36	Round Island, St. Marys
MI 13	Gull Rock	MI 37	DeTour Reef
MI 14	Manitou Island	MI 38	Martin Reef
MI 15	Bete Grise	MI 39	St. Helena
MI 16	Jacobsville	MI 40	Lansing Shoal
MI 17	Portage Lower Entry	MI 41	Squaw Island
MI 18	Sand Point	MI 42	Seul Choix
MI 19	Huron Island	MI 43	Manistique
MI 20	Big Bay Point	MI 44	Point Peninsula
MI 21	Stannard Rock	MI 45	Minneapolis Shoal
MI 22	Granite Island	MI 46	Escanaba Sand Point
MI 23	Presque Isle Harbor Breakwater	MI 47	Escanaba Harbor
MI 24	Marquette	MI 48	Menominee Pierhead

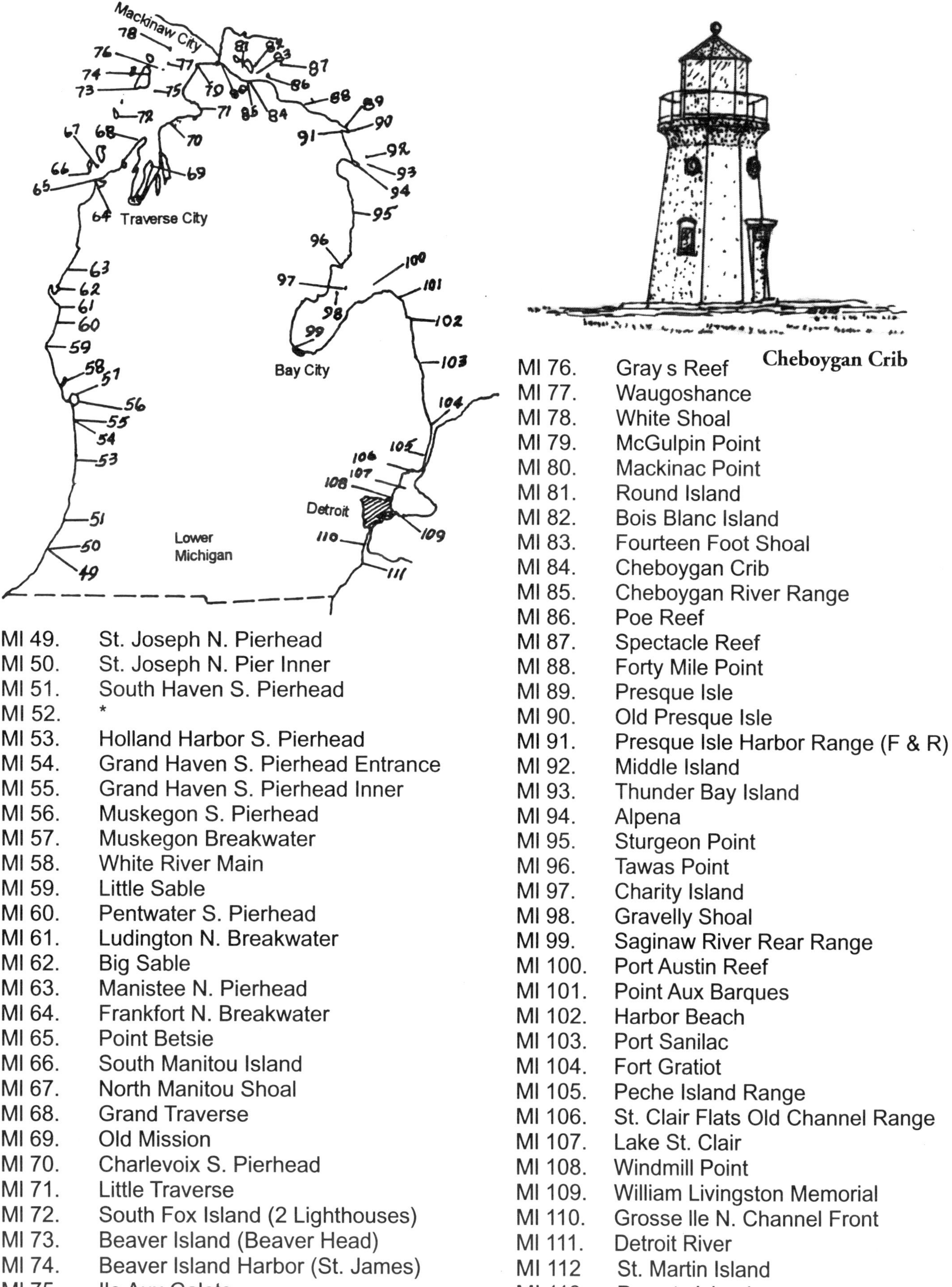

MI 49.   St. Joseph N. Pierhead
MI 50.   St. Joseph N. Pier Inner
MI 51.   South Haven S. Pierhead
MI 52.   *
MI 53.   Holland Harbor S. Pierhead
MI 54.   Grand Haven S. Pierhead Entrance
MI 55.   Grand Haven S. Pierhead Inner
MI 56.   Muskegon S. Pierhead
MI 57.   Muskegon Breakwater
MI 58.   White River Main
MI 59.   Little Sable
MI 60.   Pentwater S. Pierhead
MI 61.   Ludington N. Breakwater
MI 62.   Big Sable
MI 63.   Manistee N. Pierhead
MI 64.   Frankfort N. Breakwater
MI 65.   Point Betsie
MI 66.   South Manitou Island
MI 67.   North Manitou Shoal
MI 68.   Grand Traverse
MI 69.   Old Mission
MI 70.   Charlevoix S. Pierhead
MI 71.   Little Traverse
MI 72.   South Fox Island (2 Lighthouses)
MI 73.   Beaver Island (Beaver Head)
MI 74.   Beaver Island Harbor (St. James)
MI 75.   Ile Aux Galets

MI 76.   Gray s Reef
MI 77.   Waugoshance
MI 78.   White Shoal
MI 79.   McGulpin Point
MI 80.   Mackinac Point
MI 81.   Round Island
MI 82.   Bois Blanc Island
MI 83.   Fourteen Foot Shoal
MI 84.   Cheboygan Crib
MI 85.   Cheboygan River Range
MI 86.   Poe Reef
MI 87.   Spectacle Reef
MI 88.   Forty Mile Point
MI 89.   Presque Isle
MI 90.   Old Presque Isle
MI 91.   Presque Isle Harbor Range (F & R)
MI 92.   Middle Island
MI 93.   Thunder Bay Island
MI 94.   Alpena
MI 95.   Sturgeon Point
MI 96.   Tawas Point
MI 97.   Charity Island
MI 98.   Gravelly Shoal
MI 99.   Saginaw River Rear Range
MI 100.   Port Austin Reef
MI 101.   Point Aux Barques
MI 102.   Harbor Beach
MI 103.   Port Sanilac
MI 104.   Fort Gratiot
MI 105.   Peche Island Range
MI 106.   St. Clair Flats Old Channel Range
MI 107.   Lake St. Clair
MI 108.   Windmill Point
MI 109.   William Livingston Memorial
MI 110.   Grosse Ile N. Channel Front
MI 111.   Detroit River
MI 112   St. Martin Island
MI 113.   Poverty Island

*There is no lighthouse #52. That number was assigned to Saugatuck S. Pier before we realized it no longer existed.

Illinois

Indiana

Buffington Breakwater

Indiana

IN 1.   Indiana E. Breakwater
IN 2.   Buffington Breakwater
IN 3.   Gary Breakwater
IN 4.   Old Michigan City
IN 5.   Michigan City E. Breakwater
IN 6.   Michigan City East Pier

Illinois

IL 1.   Waukegon Harbor
IL 2.   Grosse Point
IL 3.   Chicago Harbor
IL 4.   Chicago Hrbr S.W. Guide Wall
IL 5.   Calumet Harbor, demolished, 1995

Chicago Harbor

Ohio

Toledo Harbor

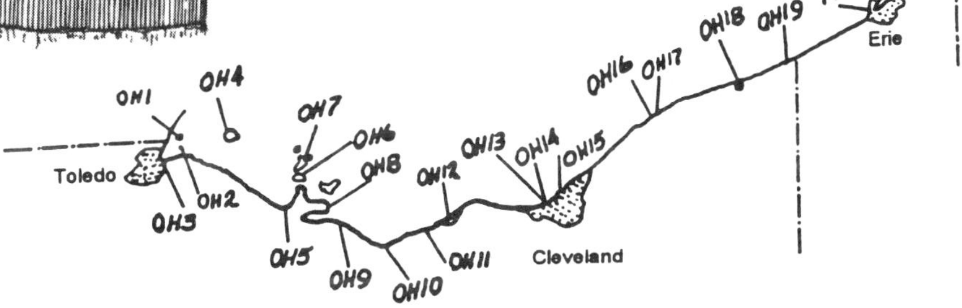

Pennsylvania

Ohio

OH 1. Toledo Harbor

OH 2. Turtle Island

OH 3. Manhatten Range, one left of a pair

OH 4. West Sister Island

OH 5. Old Port Clinton

OH 6. South Bass Island

OH 7. Perry Memorial

OH 8. Marblehead

OH 9. Cedar Point

OH 10. Huron Harbor

OH 11. Vermillion (replica)

OH 12. Lorraine W. Breakwater

OH 13. Cleveland W. Pierhead

OH 14. Cleveland E. Pierhead

OH 15. Cleveland E. Entrance

OH 16. Fairport W. Breakwater

OH 17. Fairport Harbor (Grand River)

OH 18. Ashtabula

OH 19. Conneaut W. Breakwater

OH 20. Grand Lake St. Mary

Erie Land

Pennsylvania

PA 1. Presque Isle

PA 2. Erie Pierhead

PA 3. Erie Land

Upper New York
Vermont

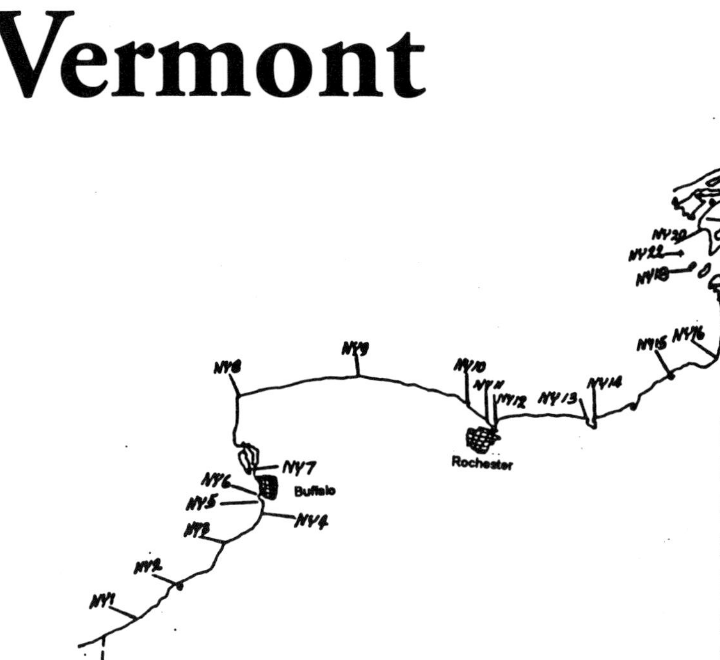

NY 26.	Crossover Island
NY 27.	Ogdensburg Harbor
NY 28.	Point Au Roche
NY 29.	Cumberland Head
NY 30.	Bluff Point
NY 31.	Split Rock
NY 32.	Barbers Point
NY 33.	Crown Point

Upper New York

NY1.	Barcelona
NY2.	Dunkirk Main
NY3.	South Buffalo South Side
NY4.	Buffalo
NY5.	Old Buffalo Main
NY6.	Horseshoe Reef, almost gone
NY7.	Old Front Range (Grand Island)
NY8.	Fort Niagara
NY 9.	Thirty Mile Point
NY 10.	Braddock Point
NY 11.	Charlotte Genessee
NY 12.	Rochester Harbor
NY 13.	Sodus Point
NY 14.	Sodus Outer
NY 15.	Oswego West Pierhead
NY 16.	Selkirk
NY 17.	Stony Point
NY 18.	Galloo Island
NY 19.	Horse Island
NY 20.	Tibbetts Point
NY 21.	Cape Vincent Breakwater, relocated
NY 22.	East Charity Shoal
NY 23.	Rock Island
NY 24.	Sunken Rock
NY 25.	Sisters Island

Colchester Reef

Vermont

VT 1.	Windmill Point
VT 2.	Isle La Motte
VT 3.	Juniper Island
VT 4.	Colchester Reef
	(moved to Museum at Shelburne)

Lower New York

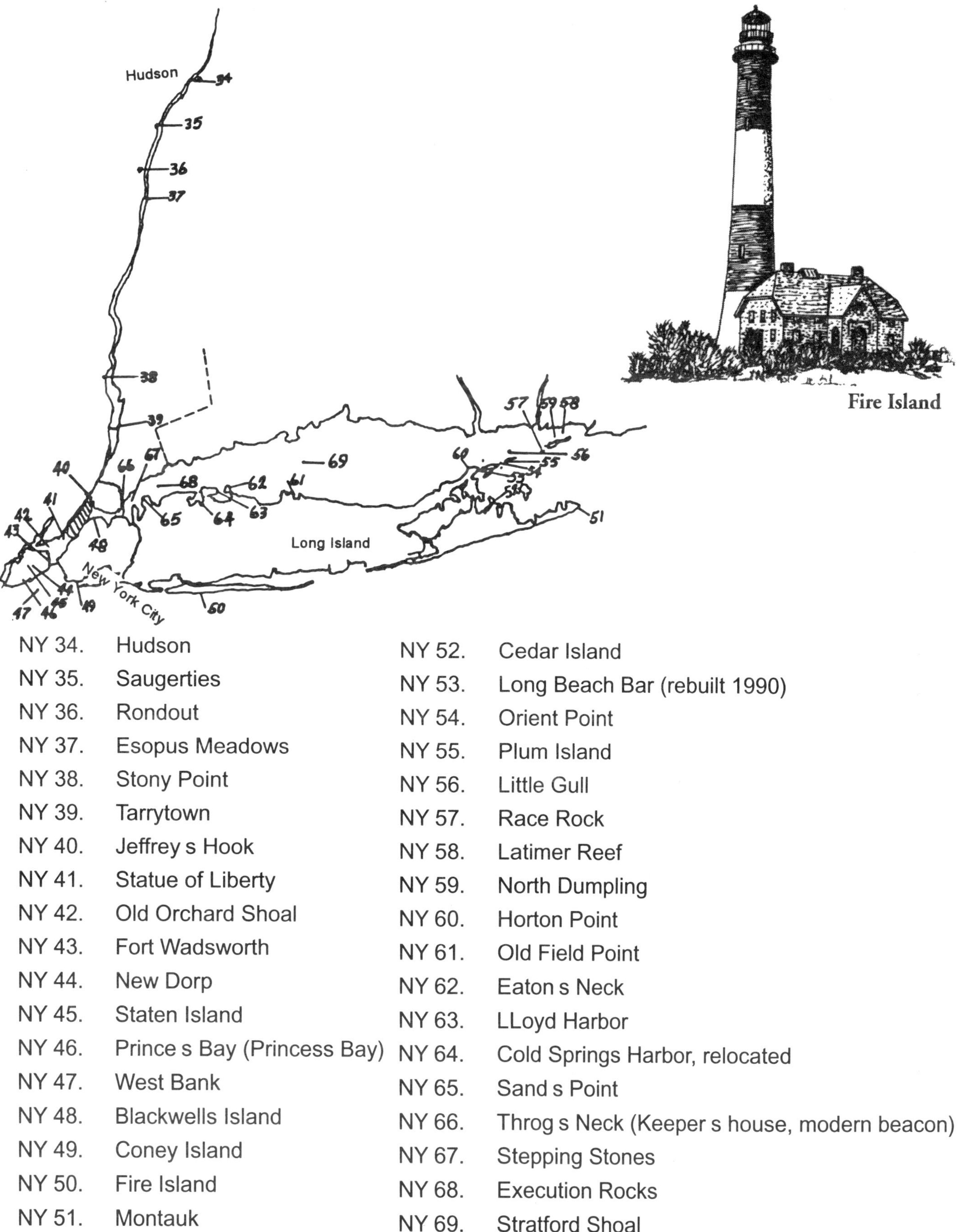

NY 34.	Hudson	NY 52.	Cedar Island
NY 35.	Saugerties	NY 53.	Long Beach Bar (rebuilt 1990)
NY 36.	Rondout	NY 54.	Orient Point
NY 37.	Esopus Meadows	NY 55.	Plum Island
NY 38.	Stony Point	NY 56.	Little Gull
NY 39.	Tarrytown	NY 57.	Race Rock
NY 40.	Jeffrey s Hook	NY 58.	Latimer Reef
NY 41.	Statue of Liberty	NY 59.	North Dumpling
NY 42.	Old Orchard Shoal	NY 60.	Horton Point
NY 43.	Fort Wadsworth	NY 61.	Old Field Point
NY 44.	New Dorp	NY 62.	Eaton s Neck
NY 45.	Staten Island	NY 63.	LLoyd Harbor
NY 46.	Prince s Bay (Princess Bay)	NY 64.	Cold Springs Harbor, relocated
NY 47.	West Bank	NY 65.	Sand s Point
NY 48.	Blackwells Island	NY 66.	Throg s Neck (Keeper s house, modern beacon)
NY 49.	Coney Island	NY 67.	Stepping Stones
NY 50.	Fire Island	NY 68.	Execution Rocks
NY 51.	Montauk	NY 69.	Stratford Shoal

Maine   New Hampshire

Portland Head

Maine

ME 1. Whitlock s Mill
ME 2. Lubec Channel
ME 3. West Quoddy Head
ME 4. Little River
ME 5. Machias Seal (Canadian maintained)
ME 6. Libby Island
ME 7. Moose Peak
ME 8. Nash Island
ME 9. Narraguagus (Pond Island)
ME 10. Petit Manan
ME 11. Prospect Harbor Point
ME 12. Winter Harbor
ME 13. Egg Rock
ME 14. Bear Island
ME 15. Baker Island
ME 16. Mount Desert Rock
ME 17. Great Duck Island
ME 18. Bass Harbor
ME 19. Blue Hill Bay
ME 20. Burnt Coat Harbor\Hockamock Head
ME 21. Saddleback Ledge
ME 22. Isle Au Haut
ME 23. Deer Island Thorofare/Mark Island
ME 24. Eagle Island
ME 25. Pumpkin Island
ME 26. Dice Head
ME 27. Fort Point
ME 28. Grindle Point
ME 29. Curtis Island
ME 30. Goose Rock
ME 31. Indian Island
ME 32. Brown s Head
ME 33. Heron Neck
ME 34. Rockland Breakwater
ME 35. Owls Head
ME 36. Two Bush Island
ME 37. White Head
ME 38. Tenants Harbor
ME 39. Marshall Point
ME 40. Matinicus Rock
ME 41. Monhegan Island
ME 42. Franklin Island
ME 43. Pemaquid Point
ME 44. Ram Island
ME 45. Burnt Island
ME 46. The Cuckolds
ME 47. Hendricks Head
ME 48. Sequin Island
ME 49. Pond Island
ME 50. Perkins Island
ME 51. Squirrel Point
ME 52. Doubling Point Range
ME 53. Doubling Point
ME 54. Portland Breakwater/Petroleum Docks
ME 55. Spring Point Ledge
ME 56. Ram Island Ledge
ME 57. Portland Head
ME 58. Halfway Rock
ME 59. Cape Elizabeth/Two Lights
ME 60. Wood Island
ME 61. Goat Island
ME 62. Cape Neddick/Nubble
ME 63. Boon Island
ME 64. Whaleback
ME 65. Lady s Delight

Portsmouth Harbor

New Hampshire

NH 1. Portsmouth Harbor (Fort Constitution)
NH 2. Isle of Shoals
NH 3. Herrick Cove (Lake Sunapee)
NH 4. Loon Island (Lake Sunapee)
NH 5. Burkhaven (Lake Sunapee)
    (all 3 built & mantained by State of N.H.)

Massachusetts

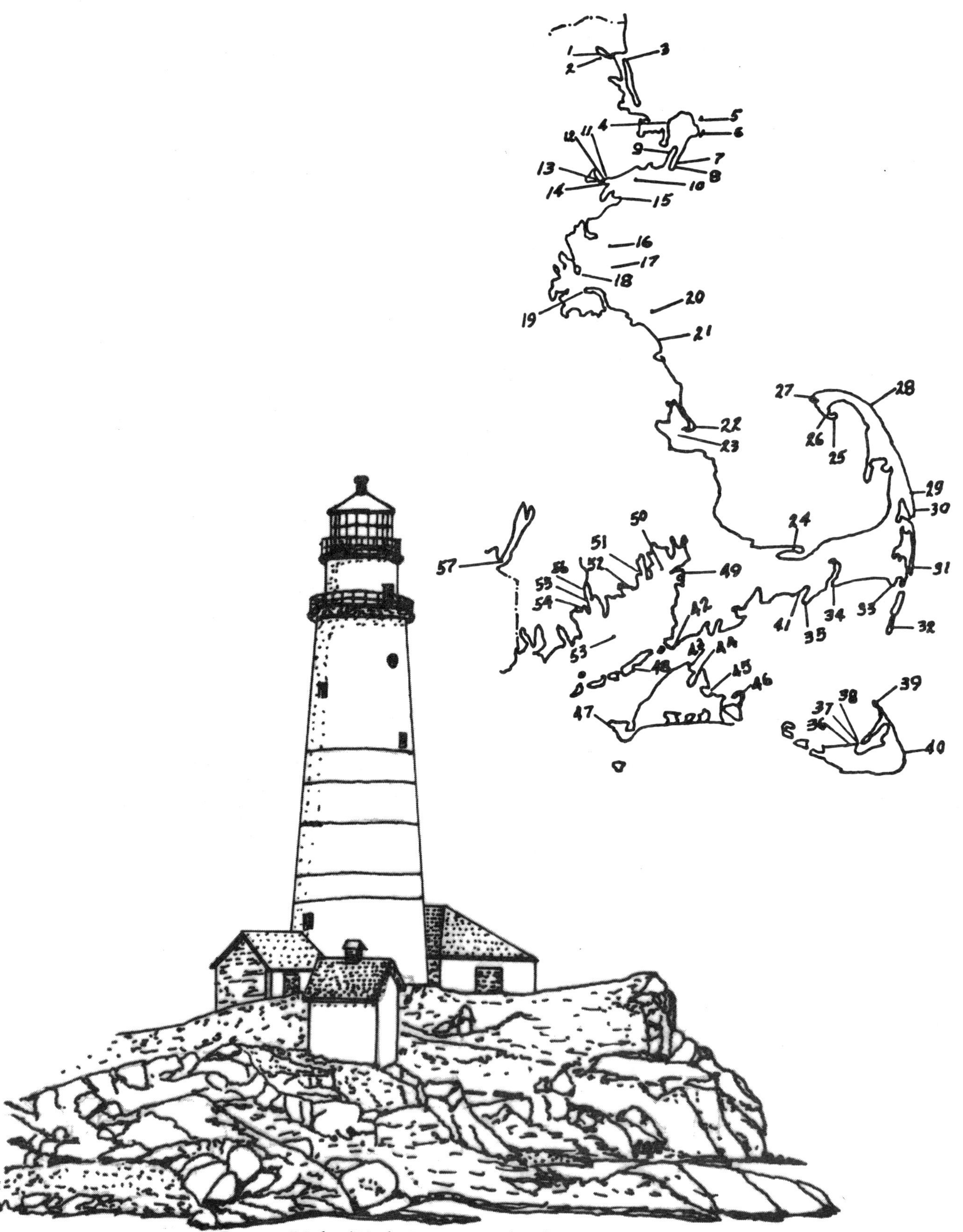

Boston Light (Little Brewster Island)

Massachusetts

MA 1.   Newburyport R. Range
MA 2.   Newburyport F. Range
MA 3.   Newburyport Harbor (Plum Island)
MA 4.   Annisquam
MA 5.   Straitsmouth Harbor
MA 6.   Thacher s Island
MA 7.   Eastern Point
MA 8.   Gloucester Breakwater
MA 9.   Ten Pound Island
MA 10.   Baker s Island
MA 11.   Hospital Point
MA 12.   Hospital Point R. Range
MA 13.   Fort Pickering
MA 14.   Derby Wharf
MA 15.   Marblehead
MA 16.   The Graves
MA 17.   Boston Light
MA 18.   Deer Island (modern modular light)
MA 19.   Long Island Head
MA 20.   Minot s Ledge
MA 21.   Scituate
MA 22.   Plymouth the Gurnet
MA 23.   Duxbury Pier
MA 24.   Sandy Neck
MA 25.   Long Point
MA 26.   Wood End
MA 27.   Race Point
MA 28.   Highland (Cape Cod)

MA 29.   Nauset Beach
MA 30.   Three Sisters of Nauset
MA 31.   Chatham
MA 32.   Monomoy Point
MA 33.   Stage Harbor
MA 34.   Bass River
MA 35.   Point Gammon
MA 36.   Nantucket Range Lights
MA 37.   Old Brant Point
MA 38.   Brant Point
MA 39.   Great Point
MA 40.   Sankaty Head
MA 41.   Hyannis Harbor
MA 42.   Nobska Point
MA 43.   West Chop
MA 44.   East Chop
MA 45.   Edgartown Harbor
MA 46.   Cape Poge
MA 47.   Gay Head
MA 48.   Tarpaulin Cove
MA 49.   Wing s Neck
MA 50.   Cleveland Ledge
MA 51.   Bird Island
MA 52.   Ned Point
MA 53.   Buzzard s Bay
MA 54.   Butler Flats
MA 55.   Clark s Point
MA 56.   Palmer Island
MA 57.   Borden Flats

Rhode Island

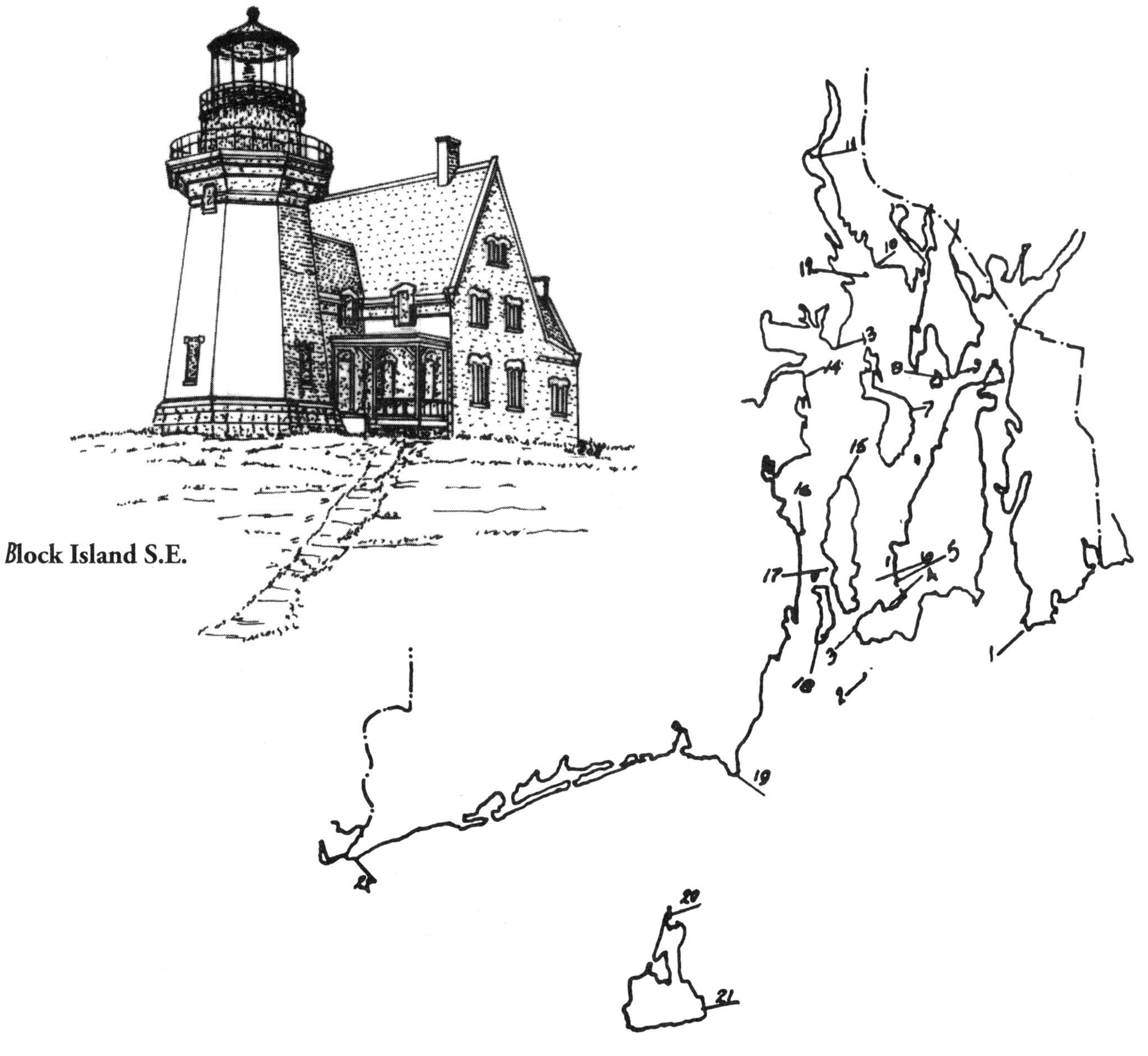

RI 1.	Sakonnet	RI 12.	Conimicut
RI 2.	Brenton Reef	RI 13.	Warwick
RI 3.	Castle Hill	RI 14.	Poplar Point
RI 4.	Ida Lewis Rock	RI 15.	Conanicut Island
RI 5.	Newport Harbor (Goat Island)	RI 16.	Plum Beach
RI 6.	Rose Island	RI 17.	Dutch Island
RI 7.	Prudence Island	RI 18.	Beavertail
RI 8.	Hog Island Shoal	RI 19.	Point Judith
RI 9.	Bristol Ferry	RI 20.	Block Island North
RI 10.	Nyatt Point	RI 21.	Block Island Southeast
RI 11.	Pomham Rocks	RI 22.	Watch Hill

Connecticut

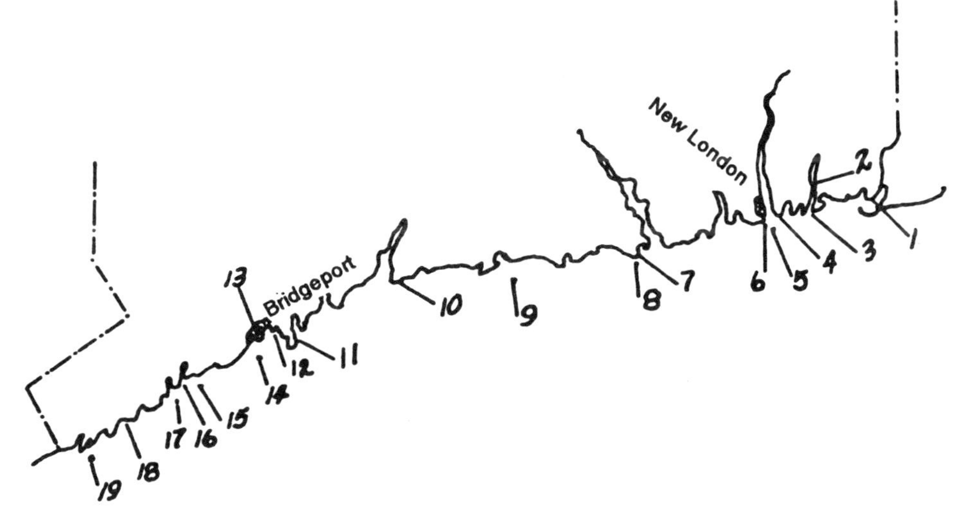

CT 1.	Stonington	CT 11.	Southwest Ledge
CT 2.	Mystic Seaport	CT 12.	Stratford Point
CT 3.	Morgan Point	CT 13.	Bridgeport Breakwater
CT 4.	Avery Point	CT 14.	Fairweather Island
CT 5.	New London Ledge	CT 15.	Penfield Reef
CT 6.	New London Harbor	CT 16.	Peck s Ledge
CT 7.	Lynde Point	CT 17.	Norwalk (Sheffield Island)
CT 8.	Saybrook Breakwater	CT 18.	Green s Ledge
CT 9.	Falkner Island	CT 19.	Stamford Harbor
CT 10.	Five Mile Point	CT 20.	Great Captain Island

New Jersey

Ship John Shoal

New Jersey

NJ 1. Robbins Reef

NJ 2. Great Beds

NJ 3. Romer Shoal

NJ 4. Conover Beacon

NJ 5. Chapel Hill

NJ 6. Navasink

NJ 7. Sandy Hook

NJ 8. Sea Girt

NJ 9. Barnegat

NJ 10. Absecon

NJ 11. Hereford Inlet

NJ 12. Cape May

NJ 13. Brandywine Shoal

NJ 14. East Point

NJ 15. Miah Maull Shoal

NJ 16. CrossLedge

NJ 17. Ship John Shoal

NJ 18. Finn s Point RR

NJ 19. Tinicum RR

Misspillion River

Delaware

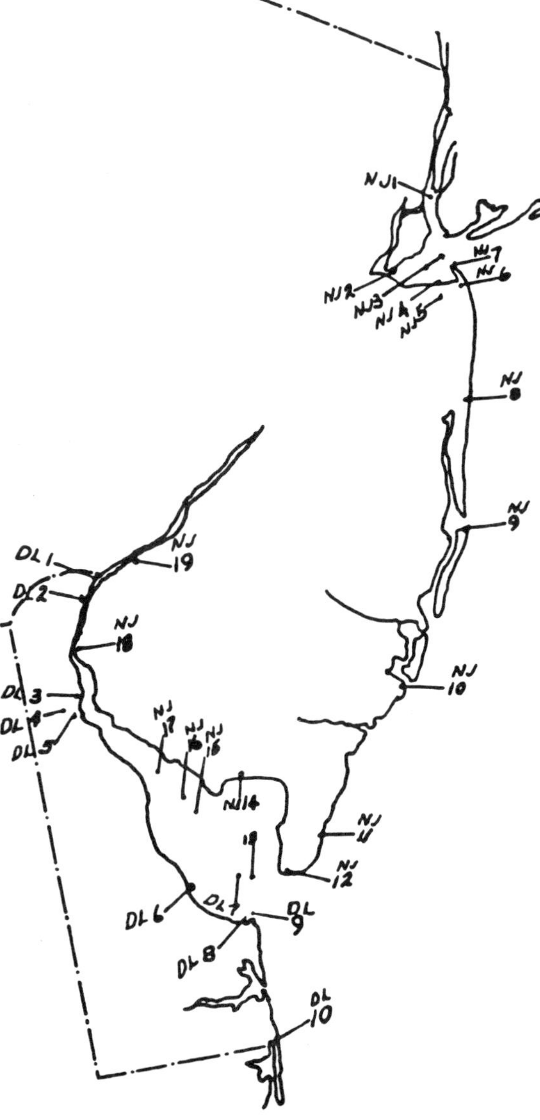

Delaware

DL 1. Marcus Hook R. Range

DL 2. Bellevue R. Range

DL 3. Liston F. Range

DL 4. Liston R. Range

DL 5. Reedy Island R. Range

DL 6. Mispillion River

DL 7. Fourteen Ft. Bank

DL 8. Delaware Breakwater East

DL 9. Harbor of Refuge

DL 10. Fenwick Island

Point No Point, Maryland

Maryland   D.C.   Virginia

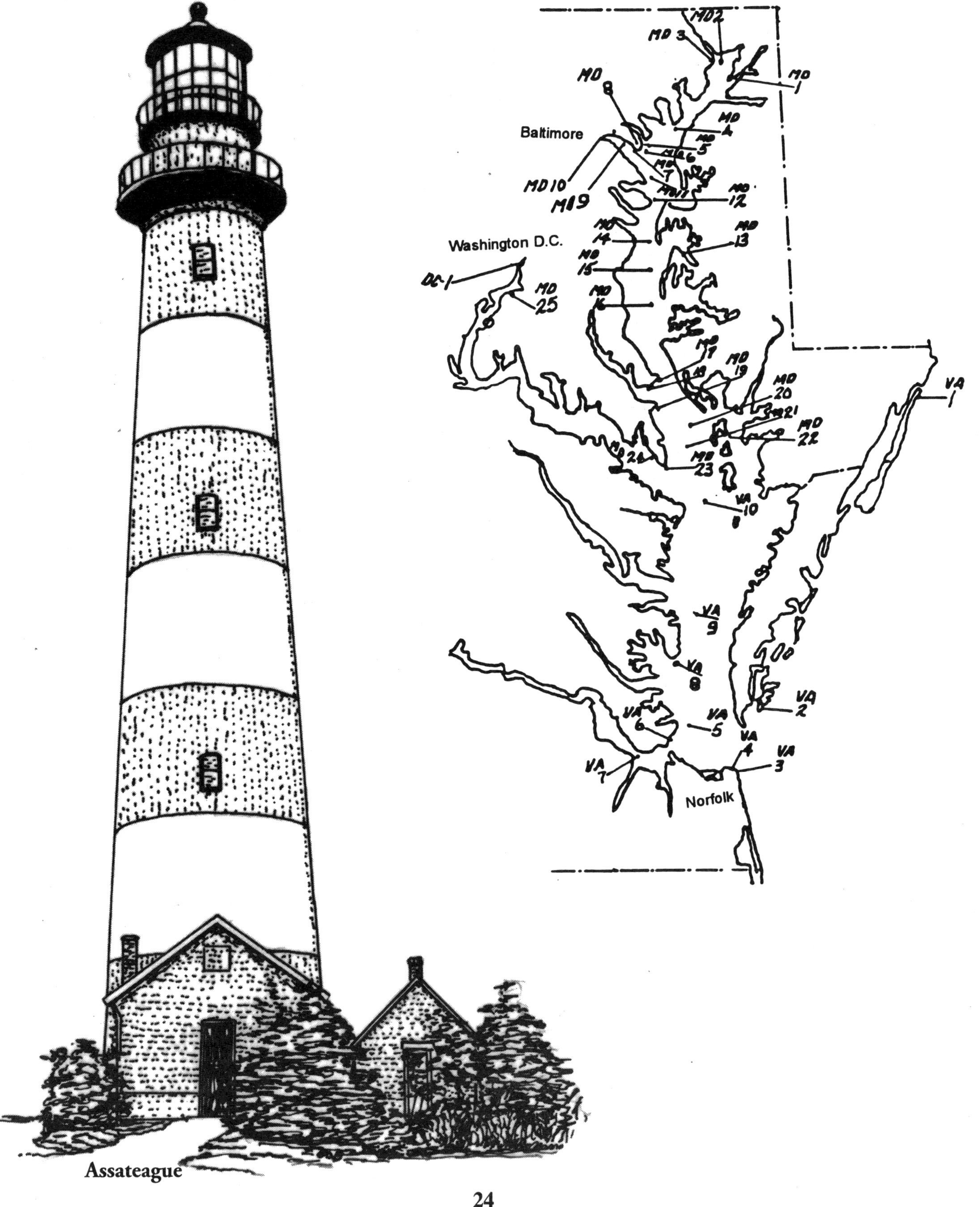

Assateague

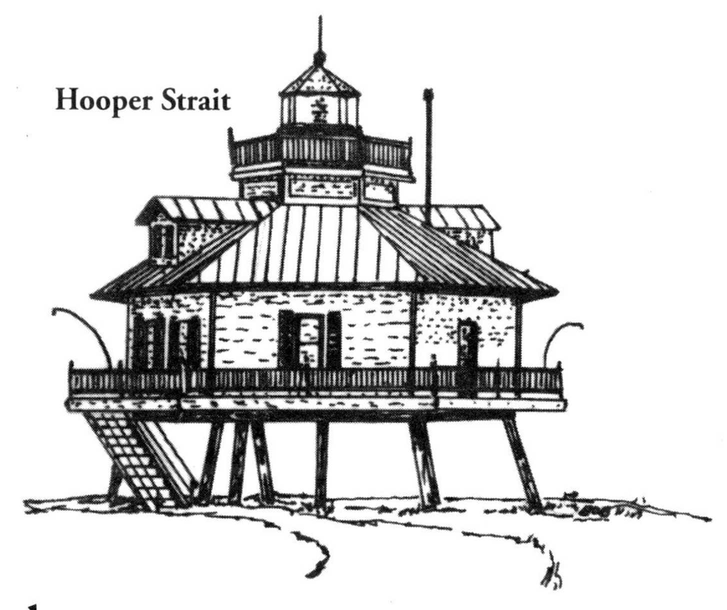

Hooper Strait

Maryland

MD 1   Turkey Point
MD 2   Fishing Battery
MD 3   Concord Point
MD 4   Poole s Island
MD 5   Craighill Channel Rear Lower Range
MD 6   Craighill Channel Front Lower Range
MD 7   Craighill Channel Front Upper Range
MD 8   Craighill Channel Rear Upper Range
MD 9   Fort Carroll
MD 10   Seven Foot Knoll
MD 11   Baltimore
MD 12   Sandy Point Shoal
MD 13   Hooper Strait
MD 14   Bloody Point bar
MD 15   Thomas Point Shaol
MD 16   Sharp s Island
MD 17   Cove Point
MD 18   Drum Point
MD 19   Cedar Point (demolished)
MD 20   Hooper Island
MD 21   Point No Point
MD 22   Solomon s Lump
MD 23   Point Lookout
MD 24   Piney Point
MD 25   Fort Washington

Virginia

VA 1   Assateague
VA 2   Cape Charles
VA 3   New Cape Henry
VA 4   Cape Henry
VA 5   Thimble Shoals
VA 6   Old Point Comfort
VA 7   Newport News
            Middle Ground
VA 8   New Point Comfort
VA 9   Wolf Trap
VA 10   Smith Point

Washington D.C.

DC 1   Jones Point

Jones Point

North Carolina

Cape Hatteras

North Carolina

NC 1   Currituck

NC 2   Roanoke River

NC 3   Bodie Island

NC 4   Cape Hatteras

NC 5   Ocracoke Island

NC 6   Cape Lookout

NC 7   Bald Head

NC 8   Prices Creek

NC 9   Oak Island

South Carolina   Georgia

Hunting Island S.C.

Georgia

GA 1	Tybee Island
GA 2	Cockspur Island
GA 3	Sapelo Island
GA 3b	Sapelo Island Range (1)
GA 4	St. Simon s Island
GA 5	Little Cumberland Island

South Carolina

SC 1	Georgetown
SC 2	Cape Romain
SC 3	Sullivan s Island
SC 4	Morris Island
SC 5	Hunting Island
SC 6	Old Hilton Head
SC 7	Harbour Town
	privately built, 1970
SC 8	Daufuskie Island
	(Haig Point Rear Range)

St. Simon's Island

Florida

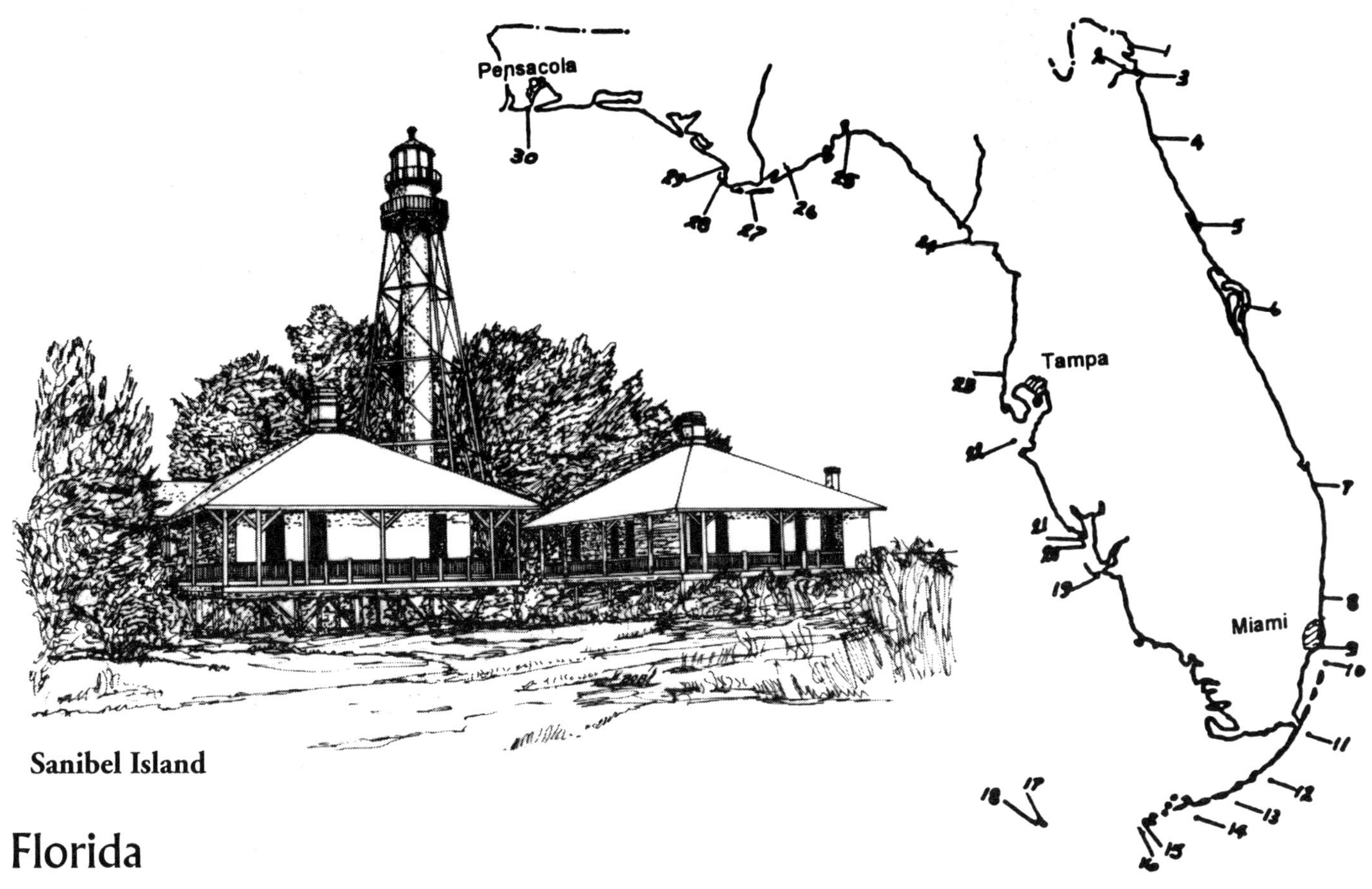

Sanibel Island

Florida

FL 1	Amelia Island		FL 16	Key West
FL 2	St. Johns River		FL 17	Fort Jefferson, Dry Tortugas
FL 3	Mayport		FL 18	Loggerhead key, Dry Tortugas
FL 4	St. Augustine		FL 19	Sanibel
FL 5	Ponce Inlet		FL 20	Boca Grande
FL 6	Port Canaveral		FL 21	Gasparilla Rear Range
FL 7	Jupiter		FL 22	Egmont Key
FL 8	Hillsborough Inlet		FL 23	Anclote Key
FL 9	Cape Florida		FL 24	Cedar keys Light
FL 10	Fowey Rocks		FL 25	St. Marks
FL 11	Carysfort Reef		FL 26	Crooked River
FL 12	Alligator Reef		FL 27	St. George Island
FL 13	Sombrero Key		FL 28	Cape San Blas
FL 14	American Shoals		FL 29	Old St. Joseph Bay
FL 15	Sand Key		FL 30	Pensacola

Mississippi   Alabama

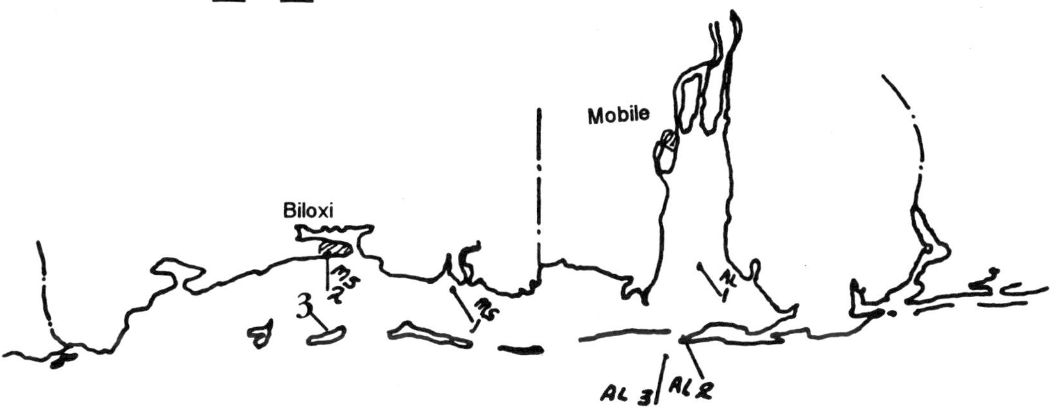

Round Island

Mississippi

MS 1   Round Island, destroyed by Hurricane Georges, 1998. There are plans to rebuild.

MS 2   Biloxi

MS 3   Ship Island, rebuilt in 2000

Alabama

AL 1   Middle Bay

AL 2   Mobile Point

AL 3   Sand Island

Middle Bay

Louisiana

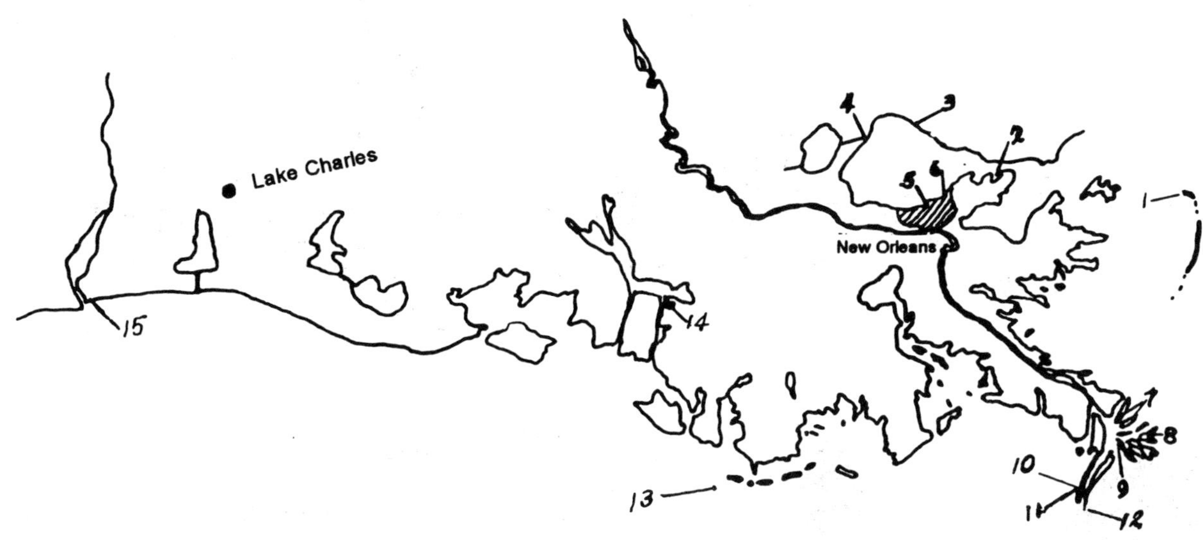

Louisiana

LA 1	Chandaleur Island
LA 2	West Rigolets
LA 3	Tchefuncte River
LA 4	Pass Manchac
LA 5	New Canal
LA 6	Port Ponchartrain
LA 7	Pass A L Outre
LA 8	Frank s Island
LA 9	South Pass
LA 10	SouthWest Pass (1838)
LA 11	SouthWest Pass (1871)
LA 12	SouthWest Pass (Modern)
LA 13	Ship Shoal
LA 14	SouthWest Reef
LA 15	Sabine Pass

New Canal

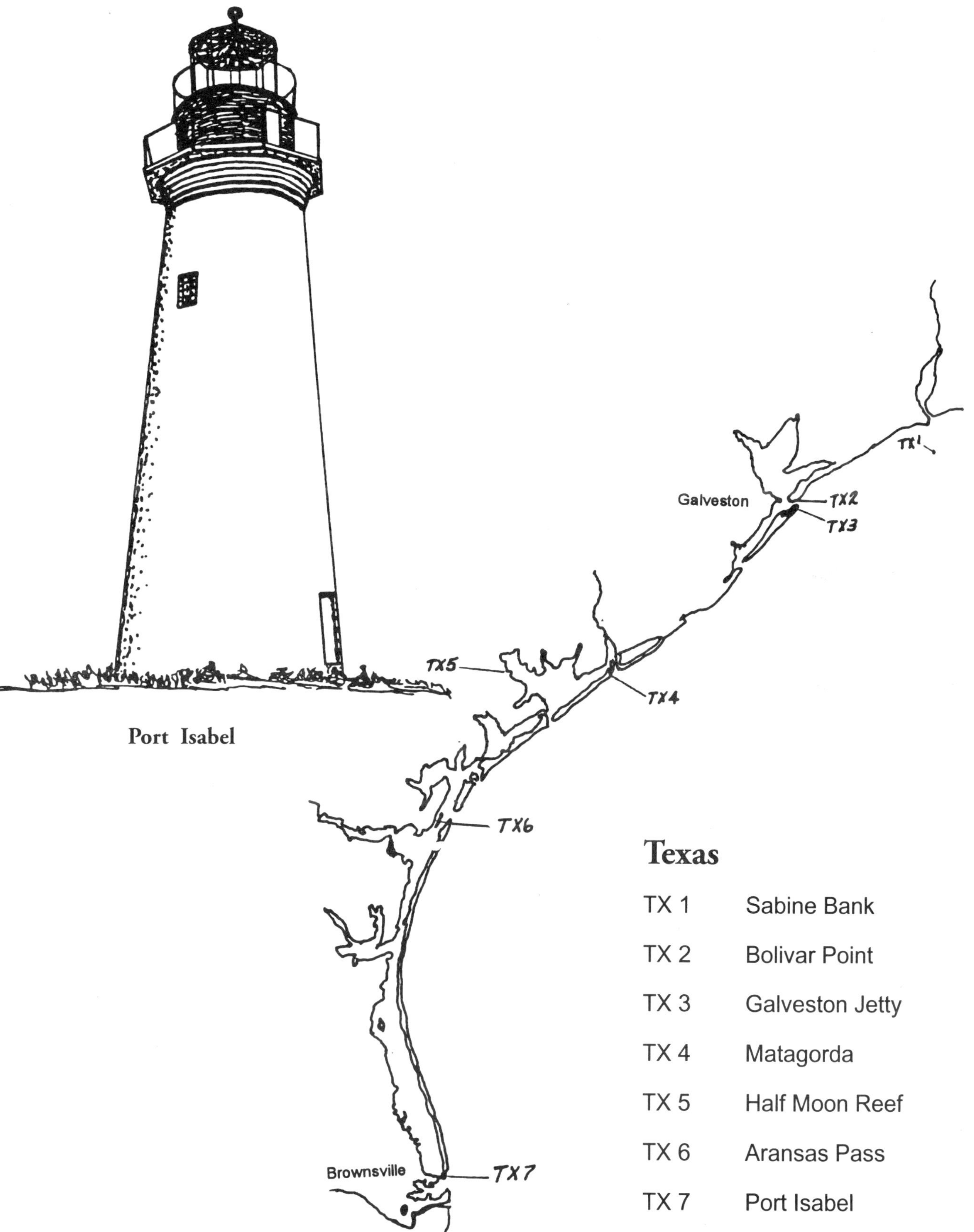

Texas

TX 1   Sabine Bank

TX 2   Bolivar Point

TX 3   Galveston Jetty

TX 4   Matagorda

TX 5   Half Moon Reef

TX 6   Aransas Pass

TX 7   Port Isabel

Puerto Rico

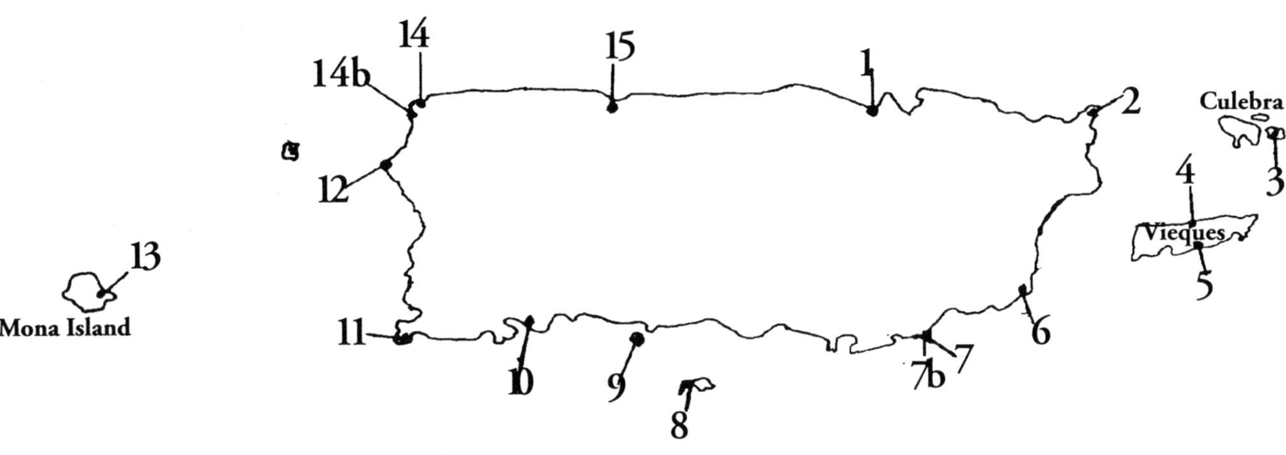

PR 1. El Morro, Port San Juan

PR 2. Cabezas de San Juan

PR 3. Culebrita

PR 4. Punta Mulas

PR 5. Puerto Ferro

PR 6. Punta Tuna

PR 7. Punta Figuras

  PR 7b. Range light ruins in front of Punta Figuras

PR 8. Caja de Muertos

PR 9. Isla de Cardona

PR 10. Guanica

PR 11. Cabo Rojo

PR 12. Point Jigueras (Rincon)

PR 13. Mona Island

PR 14. Point Borinquen

  PR 14b. Ruins of first Pt. Borinquen,
        "the ruins of Aquadilla"

PR 15. Arecibo

El Morro

This list, **to our knowledge**, is complete. It has been compiled with many years of traveling, seeking out and photographing lighthouses. There are no areas in the U.S. where we have not seen the lighthouses with our own eyes. We have now been to all the lighthouses in the U.S. built by the Federal Government. And some State built as well. Our listing is based on information from the U.S. Coast Guard, Wayne Wheeler, of the U.S. Lighthouse Society, R. Admiral Richard Bauman, and the late David Cipra, whose information and book has been priceless. Jim Gibbs, whose books inspired us on our quest, has been our source for parts of the West Coast, Alaska, and Hawaii. Sharlene and Ted Nelson were invaluable help for Washington State and the San Juan Islands. We couldn't have done it without Wally Welch, whose books were our road maps and guides in New England.

Above all we want to thank the United States Coast Guard. Personnel in every place we have gone has been wonderfully helpful to us. Thanks guys. (And ladies.)

Now, what constitutes a lighthouse, especially in the Great Lakes, and Hawaii, is simply a judgement call and not always our judgement. In the Great Lakes, some of the lighthouses listed are pierheads that are not the traditional lighthouses, but are simply beacons on towers. We call them lighthouses, because the local people in these places call them their lighthouses. And they **are** aids to navigation. There are many small light structures in Hawaii, and that is what Coast Guard Aids to Navigation calls them, "Structures". We have not, to our knowledge, included "faux" lighthouses, although there are some very attractive ones out there. We **do** include structures that have been moved from their original sites.

We have not listed the offshore Texas Towers, except for Buzzard's Bay, which may be seen from land, and Southwest Pass Louisiana, as it is close to the earlier lighthouses. As far as we know, all the others are far offshore, may not be seen from land and are not traditional lighthouses.

We have listed every lighthouse we know of, regardless of whether it can be reached by land or if it is accessible only by boat or plane. We've been to a lot of those, too.

All of the lighthouses listed here are available from us as photos. You may order or request information at the address below.

Bob and Sandra Shanklin
517 Thornhill Road
Fort Walton Beach, FL 32547
(850) 862-4069
email: thelighthousepeople@thelighthousepeople.com
Now on the WorldWideWeb: http://www.TheLighthousePeople.com

Thanks for buying our "Lighthouse List". We hope you enjoy it. We are working on several lighthouse books. In 2000, we published our first one:
"Lighthouses of the Hawaiian Islands".
This book is $10.95 + $3.00 shipping. (Florida residents add $.65 sales tax) ($1.00 shipping for each additional).

Between September 1987 and February 3, 1999, we have visited, verified and photographed every lighthouse on this list. These photos are all in color. Some of the lighthouse photos are purely documentary and not "Art". If we don't think the lighthouse you want is a good photo, we will let you know. Any you are not satisfied with you may send back for a refund within two weeks.

Our prices and sizes:

	Matted Photos		Framed Photos (Gold color metal frame)
#1	8 x 10 Matted Size: (print size 5 x 7)	$10 + 2.50 postage	$17.50 + 4.00 postage
#2	11 x 14 Matted Size: (print size 8 x 10)	$22.50 + 4.00 postage	$37.50 + 5.00 postage
#3	16 x 20 Matted Size: (print size 11 x 14)	$35.00 + 4.50 postage	$55.00 + 6.00 postage

Prints Only:
5 x 7 $6.00 + 1.50   shipping & handling
8 x 10 $12.50 + 2.00 shipping & handling
11 x 14 $20.00 + 3.50 shipping & handling

(Shipping charges will be lower on multiple orders sent in one package.)
PRICES SUBJECT TO CHANGE WITHOUT NOTICE

Also, we have 3 1/2 x 5" photos unmounted or mounted on white 5 x 7 linen paper suitable for framing, or on a good quality folded notecard with matching envelopes. Both of the mounted are signed. Price is $2.00 each with $1.00 postage for any number of notes or small photos.

Our photos are double matted, with a light cream outer mat and a navy blue inner mat. These colors do quite well with the lighthouses, and most decors.

    Please order by State, name of lighthouse, specify size.
    Send check or money order. We also take Mastercard, Visa, and American Express.
    Remember, Florida residents must include 6% sales tax.

At this time, just name whatever your favorite lighthouse is and we will let you know if we have a good photo of it.

Orders will be filled in 2-3 weeks. We are out on the road, photographing lighthouses or at Art Shows much of the time. Be patient with us.

Bob & Sandra Shanklin • 517 Thornhill Road • Ft. Walton Beach, FL 32547 • (850) 862-4069

e-mail: thelighthousepeople@thelighthousepeople.com   http://www.TheLighthousePeople.com